Relationship: The Real Deal

Relationship
the *real* deal

THE TRUTH...*at Last!!!*

Lon *and* Sandy
Golnick

Relationship: the *real* deal
The Truth at Last

Published by Persona Publishing.

ISBN 9780998582351 paperback
ISBN 9780998582368 eBook
Library of Congress Control Number: 2017909729

Illustrations by:
Adrian Bishop
adrianbishop.net

Cover Design by:
Rachel Lopez
www.r2cdesign.com

Interior Design by:
Chris Treccani
www.3dogcreative.net

Contents

Endorsement

Tens of thousands of books on the subject of relationships are listed on Amazon.com.

This is the only one that cuts through the mass of tips, habits, prescriptions, steps and "secrets," etc. and tells the truth about the nature and design of human relationships.

Lon & Sandy do not give you more statistics, solutions, and instructions. They open your eyes to what is lurking unseen in the background that makes all of the tips and solutions ultimately ineffective.

What you discover allows you to regain your natural relatedness and puts you on the path of mastery of the art of relationships.

Kristen Moeller

Bestselling Author, publisher & TEDx speaker

Introduction

Regarding relationships, you have three things in common with virtually every other human being in the world:

1. You want to – and often do – experience joy, ease and fulfillment in your relationships.
2. You also experience upsets, disappointments and frustrations in your relationships; and your efforts to deal with them have often led to more upsets, disappointments and frustrations.
3. You don't know what a relationship is.

We live our lives in relationships – families, marriages and other committed relationships, friendships, business partnerships, communities, etc. Yet the vast majority of human beings have never asked the question, *"What is a relationship?"* That includes the people who give you professional and/or friendly advice in order to have your relationships work for you. But how can you have your relationships work when you don't know what a relationship is?

When you have finished this book, you will know what a relationship is.

Insights and truths that have been hidden from your view will emerge and produce the freedom, ease and fulfillment that are *natural* to being in a relationship – *any* relationship. The nature and design of human relationships will no longer be a mystery to you, and neither will the source of upsets, frustrations and disappointments in your relationships. You will no longer be daunted by the seemingly endless and complex barrage of issues and concerns that seem to engulf human relationships. Fear, suppression and resignation will begin to dissolve and be replaced by understanding, confidence and a sense of possibility in your relationships.

The way you are related to relationships will be transformed!

Chapter One
Your relationship with relationships

If you are in any way similar to most human beings, your relationships – whether romantic, family, work, friendships, etc. – are a fundamental concern for you. We don't necessarily mean "a concern" as a worry. We mean that your relationships are important to you. In fact, we think that if you tell the truth, your relationships are ultimately the most important aspect of your life.

Even if you were to say your life's work is the most important thing in your life, your work is good for nothing if it makes no difference, if it isn't shared with others and acknowledged by them. Just imagine doing your work in solitary confinement for the rest of your life; and imagine that everything you accomplish goes into your grave with you and remains unseen and unavailable to the world. Now, if you say that you would be satisfied with that, then put this book down and go to work, because this book is part of an ongoing exploration into the phenomenon called *relationship*.

As an exploration, this book is not the analysis of the problems in relationships. Nor is it an examination for flaws and faults. It is also not an investigation to find the culprits or villains in relationship breakdowns. The purpose of exploration is to **discover** something new (and maybe even useful). In fact, a definition of explore is "to travel in a region previously unknown or little known in order to *learn* about its natural features, inhabitants, etc."

This exploration starts with the beginning of relationships and goes through all of the ups and downs to the end. Most of us try to begin our relationships at the end – at the happily-ever-after part; and the rest remains a mystery – especially the stuff that keeps the happily-ever-after from happening.

You have probably been slumbering blissfully in the fantasy that someday your relationships will turn out like your dreams. You hope that if this one doesn't work out, the next one will. The real prince or princess will finally ride in and fulfill your dreams.

Sorry. We are not the fairy godmother and godfather that will make your dreams come true. We don't have the mystical fairy dust that will have everything magically turn out. We don't even have a new and unique set of instructions for what to do or how to behave.

Over the years we have observed that the most effective actions people take are the ones that they come up with themselves when they are *awake*. So our purpose is simply to help you wake up to what is having your relationships turn out the way they do.

This book is intended to open your eyes to what you are really getting yourself into – or have gotten yourself into – when you get into a relationship *of any kind*.

We suggest that you are stuck in old, historically-based ideas, beliefs and points of view that are shaping your relationships today. Furthermore, we suggest that you are unaware of what those ideas, points of view and beliefs are. It's about time that you become aware of them.

We are going to challenge you with some straight questions and straight talk, designed to reveal and inspire thinking that will result in renewed and lasting experiences of affinity, ease, spontaneity and fulfillment in your relationships.

All forms of relationships – family, business, friendships, etc. – are included in our exploration because all relationships are rooted in the same fundamental design. However, in this book, you will probably see a tendency to address relationships of the romantic kind – the relationships that have you singing in the shower with joy, and the ones that keep you up at night, crying yourself to sleep.

Your relationship with this book

Let's begin our exploration of relationship by looking at your relationship with this book.

It could be said that in buying this book and then beginning to read it, you put yourself into a relationship with the book; and just as in any other relationship you have, you are looking for something that will benefit you. In your relationship with this book you are likely expecting to find something that will be useful to you in your relationships.

You probably selected this book in much the same way that you began many of your relationships. Maybe you were intrigued by the cover (attraction), or you related to the title (interest/chemistry), or you simply had a feeling that this book and you belong together (soul mates' kismet).

But it's possible you won't make it to the end of the book, just as people don't make it through to the end in many of their relationships.

While reading this book, you may disagree with something that is being said. Something may upset you or disappoint you. What will you do when that happens? Well, early on, if you don't have much time invested in the book, you may decide you don't like it or that it

is not what you expected. You might think, "The book and I just don't get along," and quit.

Or you may suddenly realize that you already know everything that's in the book, and therefore you must leave it and find something new and more interesting.

Or you may skip right to the end, thinking there is nothing in the middle worth exploring.

Or you could "do the right thing" and stick it out through the ups and downs, thereby demonstrating to yourself (and perhaps to others) that you have what it takes to see it through. Meanwhile, you may not notice that you and the book are slowly drifting apart.

Or you might not pick it up for weeks at a time, slowly lose interest in it, and let it sit while you busy yourself with other diversions.

Does that sound a little bit like how you and others have behaved in your relationships?

Since you did pay for the book – similar to having said "I DO" – we suggest that you let go of hoping that this book is the right one, that you will get everything that you want from it, that all your dreams will come true, and that you will finally live happily-ever-after! Instead, be open to seeing things that you haven't seen before and considering their validity in your life.

As you read this book, look squarely and honestly at your own experience in your life rather than comparing what's here with what you have heard or read before. This book is designed for you to discover for yourself what a relationship is.

A word of warning: If you skip to the end of the book, trying to take a short cut to find out what a relationship is, what you see will make no sense to you, and the knowledge will not be yours. For it to be yours, you must go through the process of discovering it for yourself.

A unique approach to reading this book

Do you remember when you were small, and a parent, an older brother or sister, or a relative or friend read a book with you? In a sense, it was an exploration. They may have pointed out things that you hadn't seen or noticed, and you may have pointed out things that they had not seen or noticed. You were on an adventure together. It was fun, wasn't it?

Since this book is about relationships, it may be more fun, adventurous and illuminating to read this book with someone with whom you are in relationship. Even though you may think you are too "grown up" for that type of thing, you might consider it. Together, the two of you may see things that neither of you would have seen by yourselves. With the two of you sharing your insights with each other, you could produce amazing results with this book.

Whether you read this book with another person or not, you will be awakened to things about relationships you haven't thought of before.

This is a wakeup book

Most people are asleep to the fact that relationship is fundamental to human existence, and even fewer really explore it. Most research about relationships has been done by studying individuals, not relationships. And researchers have usually concentrated on what they consider to be wrong with the individuals and what individuals should do to resolve disappointments, upsets and frustrations in their relationships. The result is an enormous number of tips, steps and "secrets" for changing and improving individual behavior in the attempt to make relationships work, or to have the relationships of your dreams. Meanwhile, people remain asleep to the nature and design of relationships – what a relationship is, what it's about, what shapes it, and what is common to all relationships.

In reading this book, even if you fall asleep from time to time, you will not be able to remain unconscious of what a relationship is and of your default way of being related to relationships. You will be awakened, and once awakened, you will not be able to go back to sleep completely about how you function in your relationships. You will also not be able to plead ignorance or claim you don't understand relationships.

While your circumstances may not look a lot different when you finish this book, your experience of your relationships will likely be quite new to you.

In knowing what a relationship is, and having new insights into how you have been living your relationships, you will be in a truly uncommon position: you'll be ready to begin the exciting and lifelong game of *designing* the relationships in your life.

Chapter Two

Waking up

We assert that you are asleep to some very fundamental "truths" about relationships and the way you relate to them – all of them. Further, we assert that your being unaware of your default way of being in your relationships is the source of all the disappointments, upsets and frustrations that happen in your relationships.

It's time to wake up, to explore and discover what is determining the shape and quality of all of your relationships.

In our 54 years together, we have witnessed many relationships – friendships, girlfriends/boyfriends, engagements, marriages, committed relationships, families, fraternities, business start-ups, management teams, project teams, etc. Over the years, we have seen a lot of upset and unhappiness in those relationships, including our own. In fact, we saw so many problems in relationships – relationships of all kinds – that we began to question the common assumption that the problems exist because of personal issues of individuals. In our view, breakdowns in relationships in the world are way too numerous to be attributed only to the shortcomings or quirks of individual people. So we began to explore the nature of human relationships, and we began to see that:

1. No one plans or designs their relationships to have breakdowns, and yet **NO** relationship – whether a marriage, siblings, business partnership, friendship, etc. – escapes disappointments, upsets and frustrations. So *breakdowns in relationships must not be a function of personalities or personal characteristics.*

2. *Relationship is natural.* We can see that by observing small children before they are inculcated into our human culture. Therefore, since the norm seems to be that people are out of relationship a large portion of the time, some things must be getting in the way of what is natural.

3. *No one,* including experts in the field, *knows what a relationship is.* So the endless procession of secrets, habits and steps to better relationships cannot make a lasting difference.

4. *The condition or paradigm in which we are attempting to have relationships disallows our relationships to be effective, fulfilling and lasting.*

In our decades of experience in leading transformational programs, we have observed that when what is "running the show" is hidden from their view, people experience powerlessness, frustration and unhappiness. When people become aware of something that was previously unseen by them, when they have new insight into something, they recover the power which had been forfeited to that which was hidden from their view.

In exploring the area of human relationships, we began to suspect that there are some heretofore unseen things that are running the show, and that destine people – good people like you – to disappointment, upset and frustration in their relationships. We discovered that, indeed, there are common – and mostly unconscious – default ways in which most people understand and relate to relationships. These unconscious ways of relating to relationships are detrimental – and often lethal – to people's relationships. *We discovered that human beings are trying to be related in a condition that is inimical to relationships.*

Unseen conditions determine effectiveness

This analogy will help you to see what we mean:

Suppose you find yourself all wet, and you want to get dry. There are many obvious solutions. All you have to do is use a towel. Or you can use a blow dryer. Or you can just shake all over. Or you can just be still and let evaporation happen.

Some people may maintain that some of those old solutions need updating to get the result you want. You need a new pastel, ultra-plush and chemically-treated towel. Or a new super energy-efficient blow dryer. Or an electric shaking machine – just wrap the belt around your waist and it will do the shaking for you. Or try a new, serenely quiet, meditative stillness technique.

However, **none** of the solutions, including new ones, will work to get you dry while you are immersed in water! It's not because the solutions are inherently faulty, but because they **cannot** work in the circumstance or condition of being immersed in water. That condition doesn't allow them to work. In fact, they just become a part of the condition – wet and useless – and perhaps they even produce new problems.

The truth is that all of the solutions would work, if they were applied in a condition which allowed them to work – in this analogy, being out of the water.

In your relationships, it is as if you are trying to get dry while you are immersed in water. You wonder why the tips, solutions and instructions aren't producing the happily-ever-after relationships of your dreams. But you fail to notice that you are immersed in a condition that disallows your relationships to work. Of course, they do not work; they *CANNOT* work!

We are not going to give you more solutions, instructions or tips in a futile attempt to improve your relationships while you are still immersed in a condition that disallows them to be satisfying and fulfilling. Rather, we will assist you to become aware of the conditions that make all of the tips, solutions and instructions ultimately ineffective in your relationships. It may be challenging, but as you discover what has been running the show, the way you see your relationships will change, and that will alter your actions, the outcomes, and your experience of your relationships. You will require no tips or instructions.

Actions are determined by the way something is seen.

Imagine doing this... or actually do it. Reach for a coffee cup which is in such a position that you don't see the handle on the cup. Notice how you reach for the cup. Notice that your hand is shaped like a horizontal letter C with your thumb opposing your forefinger, and the rest of your fingers curved below your forefinger. Simple, yes? You didn't have to come up with an effective strategy for picking the cup up. If the cup is quite hot, you would probably automatically put it down quite quickly – and maybe wait for it to cool before picking it up again.

Now imagine reaching for the coffee cup which is in such a position that the handle is in your view. Notice that your hand is shaped differently. Your index finger, perhaps along with your middle finger, is crooked for hooking the handle, and your thumb is extended straight out over top of it, with the rest of your fingers also crooked close to your palm. If the cup is quite hot, you will probably continue to hold it, only adjusting your lower fingers slightly.

We're asking you to see that the way you handle the cup depends on the angle from which you are viewing the cup, on whether or not you see the handle. *The actions you take, and the results of those actions, are determined by the way you see something, which in turn depends on where you are looking from – your position or point of view.* When you see something from a different point of view, your actions and the results of those actions will be different.

The way you relate to your relationships is similar to the example of the coffee cup. If you were to see your relationships differently from the way you have seen them in the past, your actions regarding your relationships and the results that you have in your relationships would be different from what they have been in the past. In reading this book, and thinking about some of the views that we offer, you will begin to see your relationships differently and, therefore, you will end up taking different actions and having different results in your relationships. For people who have been in our workshops, the results were sometimes so dramatic that it was very much as if they had a whole new relationship!

Now we're going to look at the conditions that are undermining your relationships, and producing disappointments, upsets and frustrations – the water in which you are immersed – the *what* in "happily-ever-after-what?" They are the conditions in which you are mired that are inimical to your relationships. In other words, we are going to reveal the inherent nature and design of human relationships that you have been unaware of. As we said in Chapter 1, *you must discover it for yourself* by reading on and *by looking at the relationships in your own life*.

Part of the task you've undertaken in reading this book is to unmask the source of the disappointments, upsets and frustrations that you experience in your relationships – the "blue" out of which upsets come when they seem to just "come out of the blue."

Chapter Three

Some basic questions

What is a relationship anyway?

We human beings are strange creatures. One piece of evidence of our nuttiness is that we attempt to have relationships that work and are satisfying without knowing what a relationship is.

If we ask you, "What is a relationship?", what is your response?

A partnership? Association? Connection? Companionship? Soul Mates?

Then we would have to ask you what a partnership, or connection, or companion, or soul mate is. Going to the dictionary, you find definitions such as these:

- partnership: the <u>relationship</u> of partners
- partner: one who takes part in common with others; associate
- associate: partner; friend
- association: companionship; partnership; connection
- connection: a <u>relation;</u> association
- companionship: <u>relationship</u> of companions
- companion: associate; comrade
- comrade: partner; associate; friend
- friendship: intimate association; close <u>relationship</u>

- soul mate: one with whom one has a deeply personal
  <u>relationship</u>

What you find is that all these words are synonyms for each other, that they are defined by each other. All you have are other words for a relationship. It's a closed loop. When you are finished going through all the definitions, you will still not know what a relationship actually is.

Next, you would probably resort to describing what people in a relationship do. For example, they love each other, or support each other, or take care of each other, or mutually benefit each other, or.... But you'll notice you are now beginning to talk about people's actions, not what a relationship itself is. People can be doing all of those things and not be in a relationship.

You might also attempt to say what a relationship is by describing what people have – for example, someone to share life with, or someone to count on and to fall back on, or someone who keeps you from being lonely, or.... But here you are talking about people and what they provide in a relationship, not what a relationship is.

If we continue to ask the question, you will find that you have not answered the question, *"What is a relationship?"* That is not unusual. In fact, you are among the millions of able, capable, normal people who do not know what a relationship is. Most have never asked the question! You just fall into relationships, without knowing what it is you're getting into.

If you get nothing else from reading this book, at least you will know what a relationship is!

But what about the problems?

Ordinary understanding correctly assumes that problems exist – especially in relationships. But it also assumes that current problems are the result of past events or people's past actions, whether in the recent past or the distant past. This may not be so.

The problems you have in your relationships do not come from where you think they come from. They do not originate with you. Nor do they originate with the people with whom you have relationships.

Be clear that problems are not things; that is to say, they are not physical things or objects. Yes, problems do exist. They just do not exist as physical things.

For instance, if you have a flat tire, that's very likely a problem for you. And the flat tire is obviously physical. However, the flat tire in and of itself is not a problem. For a tire dealer or service station operator, your flat tire is a business opportunity, not a problem.

Something physically happening is never a problem in and of itself. But something happening can *occur* as a problem. In fact, anything can occur as a problem within certain contexts and certain views. It is how you view something happening that determines whether it's a problem or not. Problems occur only in your view of something happening, not in the happening itself.

What someone does in your relationships *may occur as a problem* from your point of view; however, it is not a problem inherently and may not occur as a problem for him or her.

Who is to blame?

When things aren't going well for you in your relationships, where you tend to look for the cause of the "problem" is at those people or things that are nearby, either in location or in time. And if no one or nothing shows up very close by, you blame yourself. But maybe you and/or they are not to blame. Blaming someone else or yourself has never worked to make things better when problems occur in your relationships. But that seems to be the only place you look, or at least the most likely place you look. Mostly you look at others or yourself, but nowhere else.

Maybe the way your relationships have gone has not been up to you – or the others. Maybe there is something else at work that you have not been aware of. Maybe the nature and design of relationships is such that you cannot avoid being upset in your relationships. Maybe there is something that you're unaware of that is producing the "problems" and thereby determining your behaviors in your relationships. Maybe there's a default way in which you are related to your relationships that destines you to disappointments, upsets and frustration.

Look… if it were up to you, and you were entirely free to determine the way you are being in your relationships, would you volitionally choose to be disappointed, upset or frustrated? Of course not. You wouldn't cause yourself to be upset at any time in your life, would you? You would choose to be satisfied, free and at peace. We cannot imagine you running around making yourself upset – or running around trying to find people or things to make you upset.

Also, you might notice that when people near you are upset, so are you. Even if they are people you don't like, you are upset when they are. You may have a little "serves them right" going on, but you're not happy. You are not experiencing that "life is really wonderful now." Isn't that true in your own experience?

You probably don't intentionally upset others, *and thereby yourself* – at least not voluntarily – except in rare cases where you are already upset and simply want someone else to enjoy the pleasure of being upset with you.

Let's assume that you are not sufficiently crazy to upset yourself and that you are willing to extend that same assumption of sanity to the people around you. You will see that they are not voluntarily upsetting you, because when you are upset, so are they, and they are not crazy enough to go around upsetting themselves.

Not only are the people with whom you have relationships not interested in upsetting you, they really want the very opposite for you and for themselves. All of you have had the best intentions. All of you are interested in being more loving, thoughtful, caring. You want a relationship that's the best of the best – the one people point to and say, "I want that relationship."

So…it is highly probable that whatever is upsetting you is not you, nor is it others. And whatever it is, it's likely the same villain that is producing upsets for the many people around you with whom you have relationships. You and they regularly fall prey to the same creature.

You've been destined to go up to bat in any relationship with three strikes against you.

Chapter Four

Three strikes against your relationships

Happily ever after is a fairy tale (and fairies aren't real!)

You began to develop your beliefs about relationships while you were young. You may have been steeped in stories that have happy, fairy-tale endings. As a little girl you may have begun to dream of the day when your Prince Charming will sweep you off your feet and take you to the castle of your dreams, where you will live happily ever after. As a little boy you likely didn't escape that storyline, either. You know that there will be a Beautiful Princess out there waiting just for you, and living only to fulfill your every wish and desire for the rest of your life. Granted, there are updated versions and variations on the theme, but the theme remains the same.

It doesn't stop there with children's tales. You live in a culture obsessed with stories! Many of us live out our lives vicariously through action, romance, drama and comedy as it comes at us with incredible mass and speed, in theaters, television, online and in print.

Look at your own hopes, expectations and wishes in looking for the relationship that you want – someone who is always considerate, attractive, attentive, adoring, helpful, healthy, intelligent, self-reliant, dependable…, and your list goes on. If you look, you will see that you have your own images of your ideal home, your ideal setting, your ideal family, your ideal career, your ideal life.

In our own wedding, we were pretty much besotted with the beauty of the event and the loveliness of the people, including each other. Similarly in the weddings we have witnessed, there has been a certain storybook-ness, a certain dreamy quality to the affair – the brides in white flowing dresses, and the grooms in well-cut suits and shining shoes. It's as if they came out of nowhere – just like in a fairy tale – looking fresh, radiant and loving. And they were headed for the bliss of fulfilled romance, adventure, family and, eventually, patriarch-hood and matriarch-hood. But a few years, months or weeks later, it hits all of us that the fairy tale is gone – and really, never existed. Our princes and our princesses didn't just appear out of nowhere.

The Prince and the Princess have a past

In your relationships, you and your partners do not come from fairy tales. You come from – and with – a real past. And the real pasts trump the fairy tales every time. But you spend much of your relationship trying to get your real partner to be like the fairy-tale one – or at least trying to reconcile the two. In your attempt to do so, you go through a massive number of surprises, disappointments, and frustrations.

Each of us comes with a past, is shaped by that past, and is working (although most probably unconsciously) for the perpetuation of that past – because the way we know ourselves is by our past. Our pasts, most of which were not even of our own making, have a much, much larger imprint on us than most of us have even begun to consider. So much so that it could be argued that you don't *have* a past, you *are* a past – a very particular past. In fact, as you will see later, you know yourself and other people through histories – stories of the past.

When you begin a relationship, you are taking on your partner's entire past. That past consists of all the years your partner has been alive. It consists of all the experiences that your partner has ever gone through. As a relationship, you and your partner are Past #1 + Past #2. And the quality of the relationship depends and the way Past #1 relates to and deals with Past #2, and how Past #2 relates to and deals with Past #1. And if you think that you are going to change your partner after you commit to the relationship, try changing the past!

All relationships, of every kind, exist in the same way – two pasts, each hard at work trying to make sure its set of wants and wishes do not get preempted by the other past's set of wants and wishes. As long as each is getting most of what it's looking for and not giving up too much, the relationship continues. If one past begins to think that it's giving up too much and not getting enough, it leaves the relationship.

And it goes looking for a more compatible past to have a relationship with.

The problem is that your next relationship consists of two even larger pasts. Your desire for things to be consistent with your past-based set of wants, needs, wishes, opinions, points of view, etc. has become larger and more difficult to satisfy, and now also includes what you must avoid.

It is not possible to start from scratch. And it's time to wake up to that fact.

It's time to wake up to some very fundamental "truths" about relationships and the way you relate to them – all of them. It's time to wake up to the fact that people's default way of being in relationships is the source of all of the disappointments, frustrations and upsets that happen in relationships.

Strike 1 – The fantasy in relationships

One of the things that you know for certain about your life is that you have had at least some problems in all of your relationships – probably starting with members of your family. The problems may not always have been huge, earthshaking issues, but they nonetheless existed. And you know what the problems were – even if you don't remember the exact time they occurred or what caused them.

Right now, **please take time out from reading and make a detailed list of all of the areas in which problems have shown up in your relationships.** You might begin with money and finances – budgets and budgeting, earnings, spending priorities, necessities versus luxuries, savings, investments, allowances, etc. Move on to responsibilities – tasks and chores, discipline, community, family, etc. Continue on with problems in areas such as goals, values, lifestyle, points-of-view, home design and decor, dress and appearance, politics, beliefs and religion, spirituality, sex, children, careers, education, communication, family, extended family, where to live, friends and associates, expectations, interests, vacations, entertainment (music, movies, theatre, art, etc.), cars/transportation, sports and activities, pets, health and welfare, hygiene, drugs, food and diet, etc. Get all of the problem areas listed, including the little niggling issues, such as loading the dishwasher, managing the remote control, and parking the car.

Please do not proceed to read beyond this point until you have made a full, comprehensive list of the problems that you are encountering or have encountered in your relationships.

After you have completed your list, please review your list of problems that you have encountered, in your relationships. If you are reading this book with another person, share your lists with each other.

No big surprises

It is worth noting that while your list is long, it is not infinite. It doesn't extend out past the ends of the universe.

It is also worth knowing that all people who list the problems in their relationships will come up with pretty much the same things. We have demonstrated this many times in the workshops that we have conducted over the past decades. The issues and problems that you have are similar to those of most people, regardless of where they live in the world. The aspects of relationships in which all people encounter problems are the same as yours.

The problems are not new or surprising. They are expected. They are talked about and written about almost incessantly. Even though you may have wished that you could be an exception, you have known that problems inevitably show up in all relationships. It's what is behind the notion of a short period of time called a "honeymoon." You know that the kinds of problems you listed have existed in human relationships for a long time – well before you encountered them personally.

As you look at the length of the list of problems that you have encountered in your relationships – and you realize that almost everyone else is dealing with a similar number and range of problems – and you notice that *you knew that the problems were coming,* it may occur to you to ask a relatively obvious question, *"Why get into a relationship in the first place?"*

Good question! Included in what you already know about relationships are the answers to that question.

Please take the time now to make a comprehensive list of the reasons why you have gotten into the various relationships that you have had in your life.

Include the relatively obscure reasons, such as having a captive audience for your humor, or being able to drive in the HOV lanes on freeways.

Please do not proceed to read beyond this point until you have made a full, comprehensive list of the reasons why you and others got into your various relationships.

After you have completed your list, please review your list of reasons why you got into your various relationships. If you are reading this with another person, read your lists to each other.

Again, no big surprises

Undoubtedly you will see things like personal and/or physical appearance and attraction, sex, love, an affinity or a liking for the other person, different and interesting views of life, shared interests, companionship, mutual benefits such as financial security, stability and efficiencies, tax breaks, similar values and beliefs, children and family, a home, moral support, vacations together, friends, entertainment, contributions and gifts, receiving acknowledgment and appreciation, distribution of responsibilities and chores, shared transportation, activities, welfare and health, spirituality, conversation, etc.

If you look, you will see that you have the same reasons for getting into relationships as most people. And you, like most people, have actually gotten what you were looking for – at least *most* of what you were looking for – at some time or another during your relationships.

Surprise!

Look closely at the two lists you have made. As you compare them, you may begin to see something interesting. The two lists are quite similar! Your first list (the problems you have encountered) has nearly all of the same items as your second list (the reasons you got into your relationships). The aspects of relationships that are important to you appear on both lists.

How is it that nearly everything that you get into a relationship for becomes a problem?

If you think about it, you will begin to realize that you are not disappointed and upset in your relationships because you don't get what you want. Often you *do* get what you want. Yet you are often disappointed and upset even when you get what you want, because your relationships, and the others in your relationships, will never be enough for you!

Check this out. If you were getting 50% of what you want in a relationship, would you really feel you have a great relationship? Probably not. You're only getting half of what you want! How about 75%? Probably not! You would be missing 25% of what you want from the relationship! And if you look, 95% would probably not be enough either, even though you might say at this moment you would settle for that. You would still be *settling* for less than what you want! You know as well as we do that the closer you get to the mark – a championship, for example – the more disappointed and upset you are when you miss it! Your attention automatically goes to what is missing.

To tell the truth, you will be at least somewhat disappointed and *not fully* satisfied in your relationships unless you get *everything* that you want – 100% of it!! *All of it!*

Now, you probably haven't noticed that you *have gotten* everything you've wanted in your relationships. Probably you haven't had all of it at the same time, but you have had some of everything that you have wanted. Perhaps you've even had each of the things that you've wanted quite often – but you probably haven't been aware of it, because "often" is not enough for you. Settling for "often" is less than what you want, which leaves you disappointed.

Look… if you had everything that you wanted 50% of the time, would that be enough for you to feel that you have a great relationship? No. How about 75% of the time? Nope. Not enough. Still settling for less than what you want. You will not be fully satisfied in a relationship until you have *everything* you want *all the time* – at least all the time when you want it!

You may not have been aware of this, but you will be dissatisfied – and at least mildly disappointed and upset – if you don't have whatever you want whenever you want it. On demand! 100% of what you want, 100% of the time! *All of it, all the time!*

And that's not the end of it! If you have everything you want from your relationship every time you want it, but only in some places and not in others, you will still not be satisfied. You must have it wherever you are! You must have *all of it, all the time, everywhere!*

And that is *still* not the end of it. If you had all of it, all the time, everywhere, but only in some relationships, would that be enough? No! You must have whatever you want, whenever you want it, wherever you are and with whomever you're with!

Everything! All the time! Everywhere! With everyone! Then you would be finally satisfied. That would be the end of it, right?

NO! Not even that! Because if in your relationships, if you had everything, all the time, everywhere, with everyone, and that lasted for, say, 5 years, would you be satisfied? NO! How long would it have to last? *FOREVER!*

And with that, you have definitely crossed into **Fantasy**!

You probably have not thought this, or been aware of it. The fantasy is in the background of your thinking. That is to say, the thinking that you do about being satisfied in your relationships is done with the fantasy in the background. In your relationships, whatever you have, whenever, wherever and with whomever you have it and for however long you have it, will not be enough. It does not and cannot fulfill the fantasy.

It is not possible to fulfill the fantasy because "everything, all the time, everywhere, with everyone, forever" is a concept. Fantasies do not exist in reality, only as concepts. There is no such thing as everything, no such place as everywhere, no such group as everyone, and no such time as forever. Forever is a concept of "outside of time." It exists only in fantasy. You are looking for reality to match up with fantasy. It can't. Reality and fantasy are two different worlds. The world of reality can never match up with the world of fantasy.

This is one of the sources of your disappointment, upset and frustration in your relationships. You are comparing reality – something, sometime, somewhere, someone, for some period of time – with fantasy – everything, all the time, everywhere, everyone, forever. Fantasy cannot be fulfilled in reality. Reality, being finite in nature, is destined to fall short of fantasy. Your relationship, your partner, *and even yourself,* will not and cannot match the fantasy, and you are left disappointed!

Trying to fulfill the fantasy is the ultimate exercise in futility. It cannot be done. It is not possible.

Strike one! You are destined to disappointment as you compare what is happening in your relationships with the fantasy – the fantasy that relationships can provide everything you want, all the time, everywhere, with everyone, FOREVER!

The source of your disappointment in your relationships is not others, yourself or what is happening. The source of your disappointment is comparing what is happening in reality to the fantasy. Reality comes up short every time.

The Fantasy is not going away

Attempting to get past the fantasy is more of the fantasy. You are only interested in getting rid of the fantasy so that it won't get in the way of your having your relationships be the way that you want them all the time, everywhere, with everyone, forever – which is the fantasy.

People often say that going for their dreams is the driver of ambition. People argue that if they didn't go for "all of it," it would be too easy to settle for less, to give up on continuing and or improving their relationships. People argue for holding on to the fantasy.

The point isn't to get rid of the fantasy. It's about being aware of the fantasy, being aware that disappointment and frustration are not caused by your partner or by you. Disappointment and frustration are not even a function of having the fantasy. Disappointment and frustration are a function of considering the fantasy to be attainable in reality. Thinking that the fantasy is attainable is captivating. Seeing fantasy as fantasy is freeing.

Strike 2 – The fear in relationships

When we ask couples, "What is the basis for a [strong] relationship?", most respond with some version of love. "The basis or foundation for our relationship is love" as in *love conquers all!* In business relationships, the response is mostly "I like him or her" or "We get along well." People sometimes do things that undermine their relationships expecting that love or liking will heal any damage and they'll be able to continue to pursue their "happily ever after" fantasy. However, love or liking is not the basis for relationships.

Some people answer the question, "What is the basis for a relationship?" with "mutual values" or "mutual interests." And while mutual values and interests do reinforce relationships over the long haul, they are not the basis for a relationship. In fact many relationships begin – and thrive – with the partners having very different backgrounds, values and interests. Partners in many relationships maintain different interests and values rather than share them. (More about that later.)

Necessity, although sometimes a very compelling reason to get into relationship, is also not the universal basis for a relationship. Many people provide for your needs without you even knowing them. And you may even unwittingly disparage and shun some people who are providing what you need.

So, we're now asking you to consider that love or liking, mutual values or interests and needs are not the basis or foundation for relationships. Love (and its near cousins: affection, affinity, liking) may be the context for a relationship, the space for it, the background for it, but they are not the foundation. You may love people and not have a relationship with them. And it is possible to be in a relationship with someone whom you do not love, although it is likely you would have some affinity or liking for them.

Likewise you may share values and interests with people and not have a relationship with them. Also, while it is likely you share some interests and values with people you have relationships with, it is possible to have relationships in which values and interests are not shared. And the same is true regarding people who provide for your needs.

Then what is the basis for a relationship?

The basis for a relationship – any relationship – is commitment.

However, commitment is not what you may think it is! Being committed is not an individual trait, way of being, or state of mind. There's no such thing as individual commitment, as in "I am committed to...." Linguistically such a statement is oxymoronic. It is nonsense. Commitment is not an individual phenomenon. It is a relational phenomenon. A commitment is a promise, and a promise is a relational phenomenon.

The root of both words – "commit" and "promise" – is the Latin "mittere," which means "to send." "Com" is "with" or "together," which implies two or more. So commitment includes more than one. It is not singular or individual in nature. It is relational, and it is the base or foundation on which relationships stand.

A promise is also relational in nature. You make promises to other people, not to things like walls or rocks.

Look...if you make a promise to someone, and he or she does not accept your promise – if he or she rejects your promise – the promise does not exist, does it? That's because a promise is a two-party, relational phenomenon. A one-sided promise does not exist as a promise. An intention may exist as one-sided or singular, but a promise does not.

Now look...if the promise is accepted, it belongs to the one who accepts it as well as the one who gives it. It is *our* promise! It's a *com*mitment! It's a together thing. It is a relational thing, and both the giver and receiver are responsible for the promise and its fulfillment. It is the height of foolishness – yet very common – for the accepter of a promise to adopt a wait-and-see attitude toward the giver of the promise. In fact, such an attitude is not an expression of relationship; it's an expression of separation and doubt.

The basis for any relationship is commitment, the *making and accepting* of promises. Business contracts are a set of promises, made and accepted. Wedding vows or covenants are sacred promises. The original reason for the congregation or gathering of family and friends was to "witness" the wedding – the giving and receiving of promises – and to accept the bride and groom's promises on behalf of the communities of people within which the couple will be living.

What is missing in contemporary weddings is the officiant asking the bride and the groom, "Do you accept his/her promise to you?" after asking them, "Do you promise to …?" Most people are unaware that a promise is a two-person phenomenon, and they beat up their partners in the righteousness of "I am holding you to *your* promise."

Given that commitment is the basis of a relationship, the form and the depth of a relationship between any persons is a function of the form and the expanse of the promises, either explicit or implicit, that exist between the persons. The relationship between your friend and you is different from the relationship between your spouse and you, or your boss and you, because the promises you have with each of them are different.

Your promises to your spouse and to your children are unique – very different from any of your promises to other people – and form the uniqueness of your family.

The language of commitment

The kind of language in which a relationship begins is a declaration. A declaration brings the possibility of something into existence. For example, the declaration, "We are getting married" establishes the possibility of new way of being together. That declaration, by the way, probably resulted from a request ("Will you marry me?") and a promise ("Yes, I will.").

The kind of language in which a relationship continues to exist is promising and accepting promises, i.e. agreeing. And just as promises are the base that a relationship stands on, fulfilling promises is what has a relationship work.

So a relationship is based on nothing more and nothing less than promises being made and kept. When promises are not made, a relationship doesn't happen. You may have a concept of a relationship, but not the actions, presence or experience of being in a relationship. And if the two (or more) of you aren't keeping the promises you made and accepted, then the relationship flounders and eventually ceases to exist except as a concept or memory.

This does not mean that you and your partners will always keep your promises. But when you don't fulfill a promise, you acknowledge it rapidly and engage in making your next promises and keeping them!

There's a hitch

The fly in the ointment here is that although the basis – the very foundation – of a relationship is commitment, you are not committed! Nor is anyone else in any of their relationships. No matter who you are or how honest you are. No matter if you are the most loving, caring, "committed" person in the world. You are not committed.

That assertion may be hard to accept. So let's look at it from another approach that will enable you to see it for yourself.

Try this one. Are you coachable? The answer is *No, you are not coachable*. Likely you have asked for advice or coaching at some time in your life. You may have paid large sums of money for that advice or coaching. And yet you are not coachable! You are *"coachable as long as..."!*

Please don't see that as bad. See it as the truth. Fill in your own "as-long-as'es...", your own conditions. Here are some examples: "...as long as the coach is considerate"; "...as long as the coach is polite"; "...as long as the coach doesn't interfere with my schedule"; "...as long as the coach respects my beliefs"; "...as long as the coach doesn't insult me"; "...as long as the coach doesn't embarrass me"; "...as long as the coach doesn't demand too much from me"; etc.

Tom Landry, the Football Hall-of-Fame former coach of the Dallas Cowboys, once said, "A coach is someone who tells you what you don't want to hear, who has you see what you don't want to see, so you can be who you've always known you could be." However, you constrain and disempower coaches with your "as-long-as'es," your conditions.

What are your "as-long-as'es" in receiving coaching or advice? Say them aloud to yourself or your reading partner. You will see that they come to mind quite readily.

Notice that everything that follows "as long as" is subject to your assessment and point of view, which effectively gives you a superior position over the coach and justifies quitting the coaching at any time it doesn't go the way you think it should go. The coach is constrained by your opinions and views instead of having the freedom to take you beyond your own considerations and fears. That is to say, the coach's work is subject to your veto.

Similarly, you are not committed in your relationships. You are *"committed as long as...."* You avoid giving yourself completely to the other or others – even as you pledge to "love, honor and cherish... for better or for worse...'til death parts us." You maintain the control just in case your relationships don't go the way you want them to go – just in case they appear to be veering too far from your "happily-ever-after" fantasy. Again, please don't see this as bad. It is everyday ordinary and normal.

There are conditions to your commitments. There are limits to your commitments. There are deal-breakers in your commitments. You know that. **But you haven't said so!** You haven't communicated them, especially in your personal and romantic relationships. You have probably been more forthcoming in your business relationships. The deal-breakers are written into the contracts. Pre-nuptial contracts are written in recognition of this. However, they are often upsetting for people who consider that pre-nuptials are rooted in doubt and distrust, which they often are.

Knowing that you haven't expressed all of your "as-long-as'es," your deal-breakers, you also know that your partners probably haven't divulged all of theirs. Actually, you probably are not even aware of *all* of your own "as-long-as'es", and your partners are probably not aware of *all* of theirs. So you end up tip-toeing around in your relationships, fearful that you may cross the boundary into the deal-breakers, and end up on the outside – in broken relationships.

You may even be fearful of communicating your "as-long-as'es," your conditions, your deal-breakers, to your partners, because in doing so you may be stepping over the boundary of one of your partners' deal-breakers.

Strike two! You live in fear that your relationships could be damaged or destroyed at any time because neither your partners nor you are fully committed. You're not clear what your promises are; and you don't know when either of you may breach one of the *uncommunicated* conditions to your commitment.

We are not saying that having conditions is a bad thing. It's ordinary and commonplace. However, not communicating your as-long-as'es results in living in fear in your relationships.

Not committed to what?

You may have been asked, "What are you committed to?" And you may have a thoughtful response to that question. Often the question is a euphemism for "What do you really want and intend to work for?"

However there is a question that you seldom hear: "*Who* are you committed to?" And if you have heard that question, you've probably heard it relative to your family, or someone in your family. And the question has probably taken the form of, "Are you committed to [the name of the person]?"

"Who are you committed to?" seems to be quite a strange question. However, you might answer in terms of sacrificing your life for your child or for another dear member of your family. But if you were to think of someone outside of your relatively immediate family, you would more likely think in terms of being committed to something that person does or stands for rather than the person him or herself.

You are much more likely to give yourself over to an idea or ideal than you are to give yourself or your life over to another person – to actually live your life in service to another for absolutely nothing in return.

There could be times where you might say "I am absolutely committed to my wife." Or to my husband, my children, my father, my mother, my brother, etc. But if you look, the truth is you are **not** willing to do their absolute bidding – to give up your own life. You must retain sovereignty over your own life. (Hear yourself saying, "Of course!")

Many would argue that in today's world of change, uncertainty, fear and distrust, it would be naïve to give yourself completely to another person. You had better protect yourself – even from the person or persons you pledge yourself to. You had better have a way out, keep a back door ajar.

Making a truly unconditional commitment is thought to be, if not abhorrent, at least ridiculously naïve. To *really* promise "…for better and for worse, for richer and for poorer, in sickness and in health, 'til death parts us" would hardly make sense to you if you really thought about it. What if your "life-long" partner doesn't want to continue to clean the bathtub, or take care of the car, or provide the income to which you have become accustomed? Obviously you might come across "irreconcilable differences" that would demand that you exit the relationship, as any other sane persons would. To have no back door? No possible escape? That would be insane! That would be like losing your freedom! To you it would like losing your life! Really!

Trust – missing in action

Part of your unwillingness to give your life over to another is that you don't trust. You are not trusting. You will *trust as long as…*, which is not trusting at all.

You probably haven't distinguished trust for what it is. You likely have trust collapsed with predictability. You think that someone can be trusted or not based on his or her past performance. That is not trust; it is predictability. Predictability is estimating or anticipating the future and future performance based on the past or on past performance. In predicting, you are reacting to the past and bringing it into your future.

Trust is called for when you don't have a past on which to base present or future action, or when an undesirable future is predicted by the past. It's risky!

Strike three: A hostile paradigm for relationships

What is the point of getting into any relationship – really?

Ready for the truth? It is to get what *you* want!

You, along with everyone else, enter into relationships to get what you want! It is **all** about getting what you want. And if you don't get what you want, your ultimate move is to leave and find someone else from whom you think you can get what you want – at least more of what you want.

Even if you are a very generous and giving person, your relationships are about getting what you want – that is to say, you *want* to be able to give and contribute. And if, in your view, you don't get sufficient opportunities to give and contribute, you will leave – physically, mentally or emotionally – and go somewhere else to get the opportunity to contribute.

Again, please don't look at this as bad. It's ordinary and normal. It's the way it is. Relationships are all about getting what you want.

Wanting

Wanting, by the way, is an interesting phenomenon. *"I want..."* and *"What do you want?"* are common expressions in your life today, and said *unconsciously*, those expressions often have a detrimental effect in your relationships and your families.

In the dictionary, the definition of want or wanting is "lacking, missing, deficient (inadequate, insufficient)," that is to say, "I want…" equals "I'm lacking, missing, or deficient in…."

In saying "I want…", you are consciously or unconsciously focusing on what is missing, and you are perpetuating a sense of not having enough, a condition of insufficiency in your life. In the background is the knowledge that everyone cannot have everything that they want.

In our "I want…" world, what is often missing is the presence of graciousness, gratitude, acknowledgment and appreciation – *and the experience of being related.*

Also, most often, when you say, "I want…", it includes a silent *"from you."* That turns the other person into a resource rather than a partner. Even when you say "with you" there is often an implied "from you" – there is the implication that the other is the one who must provide something or make something happen for you.

Ultimately you aren't interested in relationship for its own sake – unless, of course, you are writing a book on relationships. You're not even all that interested in your partners, except as a resource for getting what you want. You are interested in your partners, and relationships with them, to get what you want. And as long you get what you want – at least enough of what you want – you will remain in a relationship.

It's all about "I"

Having a relationship is only and always a means for getting what you want! That's not bad; it's the way it is. It is ordinary, commonplace and normal. In fact, the environment in which you live, the background condition, the paradigm in which you are attempting to be related, is one in which the individual is supreme. You live in an "I"-based paradigm, a paradigm in which your identity is based on being an individual. You live in an *Identity-as-an-individual-based* culture. That is what it is to be a human today. It's about being identified as an individual – to have an individual identity.

Heaven forbid that you become identified first and foremost as a relationship, or a family or a community. That would be a threat to your identity as a unique individual. It's OK if you are a *member* of a family or a community. But you demand to be *known* as an individual. If you were known only in the context of your relationships with your partners, you think you would not be known as your own person, as your own self. So being identified as anything other than an individual is a threat to your personhood. You must maintain yourself as an individual "I" or you will lose yourself. It's as if you will cease to exist. It's as if you will die.

So you maintain yourself as a distinct and separate individual. You must be known above and beyond everything else as an individual. You must not be swallowed up in a group. You must not lose yourself in a relationship. That would cost you your identity as an individual. Your relationships must not be allowed to trump your individuality. You must subjugate your relationships to yourself as an individual. Elevating your relationships above yourself would be a threat to your individuality.

Strike 3 – You are attempting to have relationships in an environment – a paradigm – that is rooted in attachment to individuality and is ultimately hostile to relationships.

What about me?

You probably haven't looked closely at this phenomenon "I" to which you are so attached. If you look closely, you will begin to see that you have taken yourself for granted. You have taken "I" for granted. You haven't investigated this "I" that you've designed your life around, that you've given your life to.

It may be that identifying yourself as an "I" or knowing yourself as an individual "I" has you stuck in the "great myth of our time." Maybe the "I" that you have assumed yourself to be should not be so taken for granted.

If you attempt to locate "I" as a physical thing, you will fail. You cannot point (literally, with your finger versus figuratively with your words) to an "I". You may point to a body or a body part, such as a chest, a heart, a head or an eye, and say "that's me." But you cannot find an "I" there.

It is true that if you remove a body part from the body, the body may not function well or perhaps it may not function at all. That is true about any machine. However, today there is no part of your body that cannot be replaced to get the body to function a little better, at least for a while. Yet you would not say that, if you were given someone else's liver, lung, heart or finger, you would be that person – that "I" instead of you. You would still be you, with some replaced equipment.

So what is "I"? And where is it?

Perhaps you should begin with the latter question. If "I" isn't a physical thing, perhaps it's a conceptual thing. And like all concepts or ideas, it happens in thought (something which takes place relatively silently as a monologue), or expressions of thoughts (which happen in conversations or dialogue with others). Therefore, it could be said that where "I" happens or exists is in language – in talking with yourself, so to speak, and with others.

So what is "I"? Perhaps a particular kind of expression in language. Look, if you had no memory, and others around you were in the same boat, would you know who – or even what – you are? No! Why? Because who you are in life is founded and based in the past – in a particular expression in language called a story or history! "I" is a story from and about the past! That's the way you know and describe yourself – a story of happenings in the past being spoken about (silently to yourself or out loud to others) in the present.

Now look… whatever actually happened in the past is gone. All that's left is your personal view of what happened. "I", then, is a past-based view of every thing that happened, being expressed in the present. **You are a past-based point of view about everything.** As such you will sacrifice anything, including your relationships, before you will give up your point of view.

Chapter Five

More strikes seal the deal

A ctually, you don't go up to bat with three strikes against your relationships. You go into your relationships with enough strikes to last several times at bat.

Relationships begin with fear

What happened when you met someone with whom you were really interested in having a long term relationship? We mean someone whom you wanted to have stick around for at least a week or two, or maybe a few years.

What you didn't do was to mess up your hair, clothes and car, put your worst foot forward and actively make a fool of yourself. At least, not intentionally.

What you did was to put together your best presentation and act your best – whatever your best act was. Being cool, hot, unassuming, confident, etc. Whatever you thought will provide you with the best chance of making a "good" impression – including looking as if you didn't care, if you thought that would be impressive.

If you look closely, you will see that in the background there was some concern, some worry, some fear that you would not be able to pull it off; that you would lose the opportunity; that you might make some mistake and blow your chance.

If it went well – including that you discovered what he or she really liked or was interested in – you did whatever you could do to keep it going that way. And you found yourself continuing to do those things that you discovered he or she liked, and you looked for other things so that you could provide those as well and make a *great* impression. In the background lurked your worry about your ability to keep it up, wondering if you could continue to pull it off without making a fatal *faux pas*.

It wasn't until you had some sense of having the other person "hooked" that you began to relax and stop dressing yourself up (in whatever costumes you successfully employed to hook him or her).

Also, when the other person believed that you were hooked, and began to stop worrying if he or she was making it with you, and began to stop "dressing up," you began to wonder if you made the right choice because he or she was not being quite as attentive, organized or concerned about you as before.

As time went on, he or she began to take you for granted – just as you did with him or her. You began to know each other quite well and didn't have to communicate quite as much, because you already knew how he or she was going to respond or react. As the communication decreased, so did that experience or presence of being related. And your concern (fear) about not being as loved and appreciated as before began to grow.

Routines began to outnumber the pleasant surprises; and in your attempts to avoid what you had discovered upset him or her, you decreased your communication further. After a while a kind of distance, a kind of estrangement began to set in. The expressions of love became routine and perhaps even strained, and at some moment you began to question whether real love still existed between you. And even if you deduced that it probably still existed, it began to have the smell of "maturity" (like a really "mature" piece of fruit) rather than the zest of something newly springing forth!

At this stage in relationships we, or some therapist, often hear, "I fell out of love." Or "I don't think I ever really loved him or her. I just felt obligated to stay after so much time with him or her." We, however, do not believe either statement is ever true, unless you just outright lied from the start of the relationship – or during the handshake at the initiation of a business partnership.

You and your partner were not so stupid as to pledge a lifetime – or even a year – of love and sacred honor to someone whom you didn't love or have a strong affinity for. And you didn't fall out of love. If you really believe that you fall in and out of love, you wouldn't even begin to commit yourself to any relationship!

No, you did not fall out of love. You fell into fear. And you fell deeper and deeper into fear as you began to communicate less and less with your partner. Fear is something that festers and grows when a person is holding back and beginning to feel separate and alone.

Love didn't go away. Love does not come and go like that. Love became obscured by the fear. Just as the sun does not go away; it is merely obscured by clouds. Fear is a very prevalent and persistent cloud.

And you didn't bring on the fear. It is rampant in our human culture. Fear is the condition in which we are attempting to live and be related. You got born into it.

Most of the time, fear doesn't merely diminish the experience of being related; it annihilates it. As fear increases, it completely blocks out the experience of love and relationship, just as the light of the sun is blocked more and more completely as a cloud becomes more and more dense.

Holding back

In your relationships there are things that you haven't told your partners. As a matter of fact, most people purposely withhold things from their partners. Being absolutely forthcoming about *everything* happens somewhere between very, very rarely and never. Lying – even a "little white lie" – is a form of withholding, i.e. saying something other than what actually happened so as to avoid saying what really did happen.

What is behind all withholding and lying? *Fear!*

You withhold things from your partners because you are afraid that if your partners knew the truth, something bad would happen to – or in – your relationships. In fact, some "experts" maintain that your partners don't need to know everything, or at least they don't need to know certain things. The experts contend that telling those things to your partners could be detrimental to your relationships. They confirm your fear that your relationships will be damaged by telling the truth.

So you try to protect or save your relationships by making sure that your partners don't find out certain things. But if you have to hide things from a partner, he or she has to be occurring to you as some kind of threat to you or your relationship. You are now attempting to have a relationship with a partner whom you consider to be dangerous, to be a threat, to be an enemy to your relationship. It's very difficult to experience being closely related to an enemy or a threat.

You become guarded in your actions and in your communications. You have to keep certain things hidden. You may even become suspicious of your partner. After all, if you are hiding things from your partner, it is not out of the question that your partner might be hiding things from you. The fear grows.

In your attempt to protect or save your relationships, you actually destroy them. The experience of being related is lost. This is true with children and their parents, with lovers, with friends and with business partners.

There are some things you are afraid to say or express and therefore are **withholding** in your relationships. Telling the truth about that – especially to your partners – will assist you in illuminating one of the sources of your disappointments and upsets.

More strikes – the game was over before it began!

Having more strikes against your relationships is a function of the number of relationships you have had previous to your current relationship. This includes *all* of the relationships in the past – with parents, siblings, extended family, friends, teachers, co-workers, girlfriends, boyfriends, etc.

Stepparents cannot displace your relationship with your parents because your relationship with your parents lasts your entire lifetime – as do your other relationships – whether or not you are currently in touch with them. The relationships may exist as memories or concepts, but they do continue to exist.

You cannot have a first teacher again. You cannot have a first friend again. You cannot have a first love again. And you cannot have a second, or third or fourth again. There is only one of each. You cannot erase the fact that you had past relationships – and whatever you came away with from those relationships – especially if you came away with disappointment, upset or resentment.

You cannot rid yourself of any past relationships. And you cannot rid yourself of anything that happened or the assessments you made in those past relationships. All of that has become part of your story about who you are.

Chapter Six

What you haven't asked

When we first asked ourselves the question, "What is a relationship?", we were as lost as you were at the beginning of this book. All we could come up with were synonyms, which didn't illuminate anything. So we began to ask a different question, a question that could perhaps seem a little nutty, a little strange. The question we asked ourselves and others was, "*Where* is a relationship?" If we challenged you to point to a relationship, you would find out that you cannot do it.

Where does a relationship exist?

So where does a relationship exist? Where does it happen? **Only in speaking – whether it's silently to yourself or out loud with others.** Relationship happens only in your saying so. It is a phenomenon of language and language alone. You cannot point to a relationship. You cannot touch or hold a relationship. You cannot put a relationship in a box, or any other container. You cannot see a relationship.

If you see two people walking down the street, it is only your thought or their saying so that puts the two of them in a relationship. Physically there are two bodies moving in proximity. That's all that's there. There is no inherent relationship there. *Relationship happens in the commentary* about the two bodies moving in proximity.

There is no such "thing" as a relationship. The key word in that statement is "thing." We're asking you to see that while a relationship exists, it does not exist as a thing. It isn't physical. The people in a relationship are physical, and the things that they do and have in the relationship are physical. But the relationship itself is not.

A relationship is not a physical thing like a house or a couple of people. You cannot point to a relationship. You can only point to persons and *say* they are in a relationship or that they have a relationship.

Language as a domain of existence

A relationship exists in language. It is a "said-to-be" phenomenon. This is not so strange or difficult to fathom, when you realize that many things that you take for granted exist only in language.

Your country, and anyone else's for that matter, is not a physical thing. Its existence is in language. Rivers, rocks and trees are physical things, but countries are not. Countries have come and gone throughout history, and still do. The United States of America did not exist a few hundred years ago, and may not exist (except as a memory) several hundred years from now. The land that you are living on existed long ago, but the country did not. And the land will undoubtedly continue to exist long after the country ceases to exist.

Rivers, oceans and fences exist as boundaries of countries only because human beings say so. Rivers in and of themselves are not boundaries. Obviously, many rivers exist *within* countries.

To get the United States to exist as a country, the founders traveled to Europe and other parts of the globe to get other peoples to agree to, to acknowledge, to recognize, to say "yes" to the United States as a country. Had the people in the rest of the world declined to do so, the United States would not have come into existence. We would be reading about a few people's attempt to establish a country.

This applies not only to countries. There are no such physical things as states, provinces, capitals, governments, universities, corporations and companies. There are buildings, desks, computers, phones and people using them. And all of these exist independently of governments, universities and corporations. That a set of these things, including the humans around them, are Microsoft or the University of Washington is completely a function of lots of people saying so.

Please don't confuse giving existence to countries and companies with simply naming them. You could name a desk something else, but whatever you name it, you are not going to walk through it. No matter what you name a country or company, you can walk through it because it is not physical.

If you really look at it, you will see that most of what is important to you, what concerns you, and what you deal with day-to-day are not physical things. Art and music are also "said-to-be" phenomena. Paint and canvas, pieces of marble and metal and acrylic, and body movements are all physical things. But art exists only in the *talking about* the pigment, canvas, marble, etc. – only in human conversations about those things. Sounds are a physical phenomenon, but music exists in a human conversation about the sounds.

Also there are no such physical things as artists, athletes or business persons. There are people doing things – and it is humans that *say* what they do is art, athletics or business and *say* that certain people are artists, athletes or business persons.

The kind of language in which "said-to-be" things exist is description, opinion (point-of-view) or assessment (judgment), and agreement. That is why there is often so much discussion and controversy around whether a piece of stuff is really art, or whether certain sounds are really music, or whether a few people are really a family.

Relationships, including families, are not physical things. The people are physical bodies, but that certain people are related is language-based. They are *said* to be in a relationship or family. Whether or not someone is *really* in relationship can be up for discussion because relationships exist in language.

What is the nature of a relationship?

Most people are oblivious to the fact that relationships do not have particular, inherent characteristics. But just as a relationship itself is a linguistic phenomenon, so are the characteristics and qualities of a relationship. Characteristics and qualities exist in your relationships only because you and/or others say so. That is why you can have so many disagreements about the quality of a relationship.

You have probably heard the saying, "Beauty is in the eye of the beholder." All that means is that beauty is not in the face or the body of a person. What's there is a nose, eyes, lips, cheeks, shoulders, etc. of certain shapes and hues. That those things, or the combination of those things, are beautiful is the assessment of the observer. Actually, beauty is not in the *eye* of the beholder; it is in the *speaking* of the beholder. What you say is beautiful is not necessarily what someone else will say is beautiful.

Likewise, you may consider that a particular relationship is exciting or dull or lively or time-consuming, etc. However, those characteristics do not exist in the relationship. They exist only and always as your view or opinion of the relationship. That is to say, it is you who is characterizing or describing the relationship. The relationship doesn't have inherent characteristics. If you and/or others weren't saying – mostly silently and to yourselves – that a relationship has a particular characteristic, the relationship would be devoid of that characteristic.

Yet you mostly talk about your relationships as though they are things with inherent characteristics which are completely independent of you and your assessments. Moreover, when you hear a lot of other people describing or characterizing a relationship in the same way – or in a very similar way – that character appears to be independent of the speaking. It appears to exist in the relationship itself. But it does not! It still exists only because you and others are saying it.

When you are asleep to the fact that you are the originator and perpetuator of the character (description) of your relationships, you live in the illusion that the characteristics exist independent of you. Living in that illusion can easily result in you believing that you are the "victim" of those characteristics – and that you have to change, fix or exit a relationship.

A relationship is a story

When you listen to yourself or someone else speaking of a relationship, you will hear the telling of a story, including descriptions of events and the meanings of the events that happen in the story.

Obviously, the story is about the past. You cannot describe your relationships in the future, except as an expectation, wish or hope, because the future isn't here yet. Even when you describe your relationships as they are, you are actually speaking about a moment ago. So the story is always from and about the past. It is history.

Think about it for a moment, and you will see that whatever has happened in your relationships is gone. Everything that has happened has ceased to exist. What remains is your story of what happened.

Every history is a tale told from the teller's point of view. It is always and only an expression of the teller's point of view. Subsequent stories are built upon previous stories. And although a happening is over and done with the moment after it happens, the stories go on "forever after."

But that is not all there is to it.

What is your role in your relationships?

Given that a relationship exists in language – the particular kind of language called story – and that the story is about the past, what has been your role in your relationships, in your stories? **You are the main character.**

As in any story, the characters and the story arise together, just as the front and the back of any object arise together. With every front, there is a back. No front, no back. Likewise, without the story, the characters do not exist; and without the characters the story does not exist. Different characters mean a different story, and a different story means different characters. You have to continue the same story to be able to continue to be the same character – to play the same role. If you didn't play the same role, you would not be you, because your identity, your character, only exists in your story.

Being attached to your identity, to who you are as an individual, you are also attached to your story, your point of view, your opinions and beliefs.

In fact, you are so attached to your story that you cannot be distinguished from your story. *You are your story, your history, your point of view, your opinions and beliefs*. Without your story you would have no idea who you are.

Given that your relationship stories are an integral part of your life story, part of who you are, you are attached to your relationships, and each of your relationships remains with you for the remainder of your life.

Your attachment to your story, to your identity as an individual, is further illustrated by the way you embellish and exaggerate so as to magnify your point of view, your story, yourself. Notice the extent to which you have to prove your point, to demonstrate that your point of view is the right one, that indeed you are right. Notice how often you say "always" and "never" and "only" to argue for your point of view.

As the main character, you are the subject in *your* story and other people are objects – e.g. the object of your affection, the object of your wrath, the object of your interest, etc. *In your story, you are the subject.* "Sub" means under. As the subject, you are the underdog in your own story, including in your relationships. By default your role is to protect and defend yourself and to elevate yourself above others in your relationships.

Your relationship stories are quite common and ordinary. Every story that you have ever read, watched or been told is the essentially the same. Typically, the main character (the hero of the story) falls into bad times (usually at the hands of powerful villains), overcomes them, and comes out on top – until the sequel of the story begins, in which the hero finds himself at the bottom again. At some point during the story, the hero *must* suffer, must be the victim of a villain, in order to be a real hero – and *the greater the suffering, the greater the hero*. You are, in all likelihood, the suffering hero in your story, including in your relationships stories.

As we said in Chapter Three, there are no such physical things as problems. Consider that, like relationships, problems are a "said-to-be" phenomenon. What you may call a problem, someone else may see as an opportunity for livelihood, not a problem. What you think is beneficial, others may think is a problem. A problem is brought into existence by language, by someone commenting – saying to another or silently to themselves – that a situation or happening is a problem. Problems arise and persist in language when you compare what is happening with what you think should be happening but is not.

Now, if you make small and petty things into problems for you to handle, you will be a minor hero. But if you conjure up big and messy problems to overcome, you can be a superhero. You do not even need to overcome the problems completely. If they're big enough, just putting up with them lets you consider yourself a hero. And you are a bigger hero if you suffer a lot. If you listen carefully to your story, especially to the parts about your relationships, you will see the victim (and therefore the special hero) that you have been in the story as you tell it.

Like most people, you probably make your stories bigger than life through dramatization and exaggeration. Dramatizing and exaggerating is normal and ordinary, taking the form of using words such as *always* and *never* – as in *"she always..."* or *"he never..."* – which are almost always exaggerations. (People have to take time from what "they always do" to sleep or use the toilet.) Even saying *"she is..."* or *"he is..."* or *"I am..."* is almost always an exaggeration because she, he and you have many different ways of being and behaving, e.g. sometimes calm, sometimes angry, sometimes open, sometimes guarded, sometimes generous, sometimes stingy, etc. So you, and they, are not *always* a particular way nor *always* doing particular things.

Obviously, you didn't invent the default relationship story line and the exaggerated way of speaking; you just got sucked in.

There is no other story line. You are the hero in your relationships stories, and others are assigned to the supporting roles, *including the role of the villain.*

Is a relationship just a story?

No two people will, or even can, have exactly the same point of view, the exact same story, the exact same memory of the past. Just as it is not physically possible for two people to see exactly the same thing (because they are looking at things from slightly different angles), it is not possible for two people to have seen something, and remember it, in exactly the same way.

Do this exercise with your partner. Write down four or five adjectives that describe your relationship, and have your partner do the same. **Do it before continuing to read.**

After you have listed your adjectives, compare your descriptions. Notice that while they are similar, the two descriptions are different. And if you repeat the exercise, you will find that the descriptions will again be slightly different. They will be different each time you do this (unless you conspire to make them the same).

If there were no similarities in your stories, you would have to question that you are in a relationship at all. The way that you know you are in a relationship is that your stories are similar – and familiar. They are recognizable. They have been repeated. But be clear that the stories will not be exactly the same. You and your partner will not have exactly the same thoughts about anything.

So a relationship is actually not *a* story. A relationship is *two* stories, *two similar stories*. And you and your partner are attached to your stories, subtly or aggressively trying to persuade each other and others that your version is the true story – arguing for being the bigger victim and the bigger hero.

Welcome to the nature of relationships!

So what is a relationship?

What you have seen so far is that a relationship happens in language as two stories. Your relationships are all about you getting what you want, being afraid that you won't, and being destined to disappointment.

At the beginning of this is a book we said that if you found out nothing else, you would find out what a relationship is. Well, here is the answer to the question, "What is a relationship?" Here is what a relationship is.

A relationship is two similar, repetitive stories,
- **Entered into and attached to**
- **In a futile attempt to satisfy all personal wants,**
- **Shaped by fear,**
- **From which there is no escape.**

Test it. Check it out against your own experience. It will pass the test.

Chapter Seven

This is it!

A relationship is two similar, repetitive stories, entered into and attached to in a futile attempt to satisfy all personal wants, shaped by fear, from which there is no escape.

This is what a relationship is. This is all it is. It is what you live every day. Attempting to fix it, change it or escape it is just part of it, part of the story. More hope. More fantasy. More looking for someone who will save you from the mundane and the ordinary and fulfill your fantasy-based hopes and dreams. More waiting for your prince or princess – who, by the way, is hoping you are the prince or princess who will finally fulfill all his or her hopes and dreams. You are interested in something different only to the extent you think that you may finally fulfill the fantasy and have it all!

If you find yourself arguing with this, or trying to find a flaw in it, or looking for a way out of it, you are probably struggling to maintain your attachment to your happily-ever-after fantasy of relationship, whether it's a romantic, family or business relationship. Your attempt to escape the nature and design of relationships merely demonstrates the nature and design of relationships. You are struggling to attain your fantasy – getting everything you want (or should have), all the time, everywhere, in all your relationships, forever.

This is the way it is. Your relationships are past-based, repetitive stories which you entered and attached yourself to in order to satisfy your personal wants, shaped by your fears, from which you cannot escape. That is to say, each and every relationship you have or have had stays with you for your entire life. You may not readily recall each and every one, but each and every one is still there with you somewhere in your memory – your *story*.

You will keep trying to make your relationships fulfill your fantasy. You will continue to try to fix them when they don't. And as you realize that you cannot fix them enough, you will consider looking for other relationships or ending a current relationship and starting another that you think will provide you with more of what you want. All of this is not going away. It is the way it is. It is the relationship game. There is no other relationship game in town. This is what you were born into. This is what you got. This is all there is. This is it.

Arguing with it will make no difference. In fact, you would be arguing only to perpetuate your hope that you will get everything you want, that your fantasy will eventually be fulfilled, that you will live happily ever after. The fantasy has been running your relationship with your relationships. It is an automatic way of thinking and wishing and wanting. Be clear that the fantasy is not a Disneyesque image. The fantasy is *all of it, all the time, everywhere, with everyone, forever!*

Now, you may not be ready for this, however, it's about time you hear it whether you're ready or not. *Your relationships do not mean anything.* That is to say, there is no inherent meaning in relationships. They do not mean anything about you. They do not mean anything about others. They do not mean anything about your relationships. Your relationships are what they are. They're not going anywhere and they don't mean anything.

You might as well get it now. Your relationships are stories. Each one is a reaction to what is missing in your life. It's a default mechanism. You didn't invent it. You were born into it. It happens automatically, by default, just as the default computer program that has been installed in the computer by others operates when you turn on your computer. It just goes into that mode. And you go into the automatic default mode of relationship which was begun a long time ago, and you simply re-enact it.

And that's the way it is. **THIS IS IT!!** Your relationships are what relationships look like. Your relationships are what relationships are.

There are no secrets. A "good" relationship is a story in which you are getting a lot of what you want. A "bad" relationship is a story about why you haven't reached the fantasy. There is no happily ever after. This is what relationships are. Nothing more and nothing less. There is nothing else to get. There are no 5 secrets or 7 habits or 12 steps to getting there. There is nowhere to get. This is all that relationships are. There's nothing more to get about it.

So what…is different?

Nothing. Nothing has changed except that you are now awake to what a relationship is. The cause of disappointments, upsets and frustrations in your relationships is no longer a mystery. You are no more at fault in your relationships than any other human being on this earth. And you are no more the victim in your relationships than anyone else.

Now what?

Now that you know what a relationship is, let's look at your relationship with relationships.

Knowing what a relationship is does not change anything about your relationships. It does not mean that you and your relationships will be different. It does not mean that your relationships will improve or worsen. And it surely does not mean that you will live happily ever after.

However, you cannot change the fact that you now know what a relationship is any more than you can change yesterday's weather or a thought you had a moment ago. You are now awake to what a relationship is, and you cannot change that.

Cheer up! The fact that you cannot change things does not mean things will not change. Change happens. Change is inevitable whether you like it or not, whether or not you wish it were different, whether or not you resist it. As a matter of fact, the less you are consumed with changing things, the more you notice that things are changing quite naturally. And as you begin to see things you have not seen before, you become aware of the changes that are taking place.

In some cases you have been working so hard at changing yourself, changing your partners, and changing your relationships, you haven't noticed that they are already changing by themselves. In fact, it could be said that the more you work at changing things, the more you are holding them in place for yourself.

Relax! Now that you see the nature and design of relationships in a way you haven't before, you'll begin to notice the changes that are naturally taking place – in you, in others and in your relationships.

In the words of the Beatles, "**Let It Be**."

If you must *do* something, "*Have* It Be." That is to say, choose for it to be the way it is.

Let's clear up a common misunderstanding. Most people, including some dictionary editors, have choice and option as synonyms. They are not. They are two different animals, so to speak – actually two different species! Choice is action. Option is no action.

Where you have options, you have no action happening. Where you have choice, you have action (choosing) happening. You do not need an option to have a choice, to take action, to choose. You simply choose what is; you choose the way it is. At that moment you are in action with the way things are instead of avoiding, being upset and being a victim.

There is really nothing that you have to do. Just allow yourself to be aware of your need to have it your way in your relationships, your tendency to not communicate your "as-long-as'es," your tendency to compare what is happening in your relationship with your fantasy of what should be happening, and your tendency to strategize to avoid what you fear. Then see what happens.

You may begin to experience being more at ease, with a sense of freedom and peace. As you become more and more awake to your automatic ways of being in your relationships, you may begin to notice possibilities and opportunities that you did not see before. And as you see these additional possibilities, you may notice that your actions are beginning to be correlated with these possibilities – and that your experience of being related is expanding.

Relationships...normal and natural

As your experience of being related in your relationships expands, we expect that you will also begin to notice that the experience of being related is quite natural – even though it may not be usual or broadly experienced by most people. You may begin to see that everything in the world is in its place, in relationship to all that is around it. You may find yourself experiencing your relationship with all that surrounds you, including with people who are not necessarily experiencing their relationship with you.

As you allow yourself to experience being an ordinary human being in ordinary relationships, you will begin to notice that your everyday ordinary experience of being "out of relationship" with people is giving way to an experience of being related to others quite naturally. You will find yourself moving from being normal (an individual working on your relationships) to being natural (an individual expressing your relationships with others).

You may begin to experience that relationship is natural, even though "out-of-relationship" is very normal.

Chapter Eight

Now that you are awake

When you are awake to what a relationship is, nothing is different – except that, when you are no longer fighting or resisting the way relationships are, you may begin to see that they are changing quite naturally, even though some changes happen so slowly and in such small increments that you ordinarily fail to notice them.

Your relationships still have no inherent meaning. They don't mean anything – about you, the others or life. They just are what they are.

Meaning and mattering

That relationships do not mean anything, that they don't have any inherent significance, does not mean that relationships don't matter.

People often confuse meaning and mattering. We hear people say, "It doesn't matter" when they intend to convey, "It doesn't mean anything." Matter has to do with physical stuff. Meaning has to do with point of view or interpretation.

Let's illustrate the difference.

If you hold a tissue box over your head, it doesn't mean anything. It's just there. However, it matters. You must reach up to get a tissue. And if you drop the box to the floor, it doesn't mean anything. However, it matters because now you must bend over and reach down

67

to get a tissue. Bending over doesn't mean anything. However, it matters because your shirt may become untucked from your trousers. That your shirt becomes untucked doesn't mean anything. However, it matters because you must now…etc.

So while relationships do not mean anything, they matter. Certain things can be created and accomplished within a relationship that cannot be created and accomplished by an individual. An example of that is the conception of a child.

Relationships don't mean anything – and they matter.

Transcending normal relationships

Transcendence is often linked with a state of bliss – something akin to "leaving the world behind and experiencing other-worldliness." It is often associated with escaping the travails or routine of everyday ordinary life and ascending into bliss.

While that's a very romantic notion – and a "space" often sought by people – we'd like you to consider that the nature of transcendence is expansion rather than ascension. Transcending something does not mean leaving that thing behind. As a mentor of ours once said, "Transcendence includes that which is transcended." That is to say, transcending is not about escaping something.

Transcending ordinary, normal relationships is not about escaping ordinary, normal relationships. It's about allowing ordinary relationships to be the way they are and allowing new experiences of relationship to emerge as well. **When you are no longer working at changing or fixing ordinary relationships, you have room to experience the extraordinariness of relationship – and of your relationships.**

Trust – a gift

Trust is not prediction, which is based on the past. Trust is the very opposite of prediction. It is future-based. *Despite someone's past performance, or not knowing it,* you are willing to trust him or her for a particular future performance. Prediction is a calculation. Trust is a creation that allows for an unpredictable future.

Trusting is sometimes thought of as naive or foolish. However, trusting has real power because it allows for a future that is not determined by the past. At any moment, you are either trusting – trusting yourself, others and life – or not.

Trust is a gift that you give to yourself and others – the gift of a possible future that is not determined by the past.

To say that you cannot trust someone is a lie. You are able – you have the power – to trust at any time under any circumstance. The only question is, "Are you going to trust or not?" Either response, either yes or no, is okay. Just don't lie about it.

A "new" language for relationships

It is now clear that your relationships are not physical things. Your relationships exist in language as stories of the past – in your thoughts and in your conversations with others.

Let's now look at a relationship from another point of view and consider that while you cannot dissociate relationship from language, a relationship can also exist in another kind of language. It can exist in the language of the present and future. As we said in Chapter Four, relationships begin with a statement or declaration. It could be as simple as the statement, "We are going to date only each other." Or "We are going to build a bridge together."

A declaration does not proclaim a fact (that's the job of the kind of language called an assertion, which requires some evidence or proof of the fact). A declaration proclaims a possibility. Thus, a relationship begins as a possibility. A declaration produces the existence of the possibility of a relationship, or, said another way, it produces a relationship as a possibility, not as a fact.

To illustrate, let's look at what is popularly called The Declaration of Independence, a document actually named The Declaration of the Thirteen United States of America. That declaration was not about separating some people from others. That declaration brought into existence the possibility of a country called the United States of America. The founding fathers then went to other peoples in the world and asked them to recognize the United States of America as a country. It was when those other peoples (countries) *promised* to do so that the United States of America became a country, *in fact or reality.*

The kind of language in which a relationship begins – and continues – to exist *as a fact or reality* (in addition to existing as a possibility) is promising. A marriage becomes a fact when two persons *promise* to love, honor and cherish each other and an officiant acknowledges the giving and accepting of the promises, at which time the officiant *declares* the people married. That declaration creates a *possible* future which did not exist before the declaration. And the marriage exists as a fact or reality as a function of promises given, accepted and kept.

When two people sign a business contract – when they agree to a set of promises – their relationship shifts from being a possibility to being a fact or reality. And the proclamation of that set of promises creates a new possible future for others.

Just as an agreement (a set of promises) is what a relationship is, keeping agreements (the promises) is what has a relationship thrive. It is that simple! When promises are not kept – and it is likely some will not be – the relationship goes into breakdown and must be revived with the acknowledgment of the broken promises and the making of new promises. If that does not happen, the relationship ceases to exist as anything but a concept. The experience of being related dissipates. If you look, this is true for individuals, groups, communities, states and nations.

The kind of language that translates possibilities into realities by initiating promises is requesting. You may find it difficult to make requests because requests are acts of responsibility for moving possibilities to realities. Requests and promises are linguistic actions that take you to the future, beyond past-based stories – reasons, explanations and excuses.

The quality of a relationship

While it may appear that the quality of your relationships is a function of actions or behaviors, that is an illusion. The quality of your relationships is actually determined by the way you *describe* the actions and behaviors. If you describe certain actions and behaviors in your relationship as exciting, then you have an exciting relationship. If you describe those same actions and behaviors as boring, then you have a boring relationship. If you describe them as interesting, you have an interesting relationship.

It could be said that the quality of your relationships exists in your mouth. The quality of your relationships exists as a function of what you say it to be.

Common concerns in relationships

Sex is often an issue in certain kinds of relationships. For now, all you need to know about sex is that it is an activity. It has nothing to do with relationship *inherently*. Your partners and you may link sex to relationship – many, if not most, of the people in our culture have done so – but sex and relationship are not inherently connected. If you do link them together, you do so by promises, and those promises become a part of the design of your relationship.

Money is also often an issue. Money may appear to be connected to relationship because both are based on promises. Also, money has become a "stand-in" for almost everything, including personal worth or value. However, relationship and money are not inherently related. Ultimately, it is up to your partners and you to make and accept promises regarding money and then fulfill those promises.

Time is also an issue in many relationships. However, the amount of time you spend together is not an inherent indicator of the quality of your relationships. Neither are other "indicators" such as touching, feeling, appearance, listening, etc. Your partners and you can agree – via requests and promises – to make them indicators, but it's creating together, making and fulfilling requests and promises, that produces the closeness, aliveness and fulfillment in your relationships.

Another design for relationships

A relationship exists in language. When you are *talking about* a relationship, it is a *story* from and about the past – a history. When you are *living* a relationship, it *is a set of declarations, requests and promises* in the present for the future.

There is another familiar and common phenomenon in our lives that has the same character as a relationship – that is to say it is a story when you talk about it and a set of declarations, requests and promises being fulfilled when you are actively engaged in it. It's called a *game*.

When you look closely, a relationship has all the characteristics of a game. In fact it could be said that a relationship *is* a game. And if you design and play your relationship as a game, you might find that it works extraordinarily well, and provides you with all the benefits that you obtain from playing a game – including fun, joy and satisfaction.

However, to play effectively, you must understand the nature and design of games.

Chapter Nine

A game worth playing

The nature of games

As with games, when you see relationships for what they are and how they are designed, you are free to *play* and to play *effectively*.

The first thing to see about games is that they are completely arbitrary! There is no grand scheme behind the design of the game called basketball. Its rules, and the rules of any other game, are made up arbitrarily.

The second thing to understand is that games don't *have* rules; games *are* their rules. Basketball and Monopoly are their rules. No rules, no game. If you are *not* playing according to the rules, you are *not* playing the game. It could be said that you have never cheated in a game. You simply stopped playing the game when you stopped playing according to the rules.

The third thing to know is that games don't mean anything; there is no inherent meaning in playing a game. However, playing a game matters. Basketball doesn't mean anything – and it matters to a lot of people, including people who are gaining physical prowess and people who get paid for playing. Games are not frivolous.

The design of games

Children are good at making up and playing games because their games do not have to be significant or sophisticated. Also, they are not attached to winning. When adults are asked what the point of playing a game is, almost all of them say it is winning. Young children don't see winning as the point of playing a game. Children benefit simply by playing. They experience joy and fun; they learn; they gain skills. And that may be the real point of playing a game: gaining skills, experiences and memories. You cannot help but gain those things, even when you "lose."

In designing a game with people who see the benefit of playing a game, even if they may not know exactly what it looks like, you first discover and align on what you want to gain in playing the game – what goals the players are interested in attaining. In all probability, you are going to come up with these goals when you examine the values you have in life. Powerful purposes, goals and principles for playing are derived from your basic values – and from the ways of being that inspire and enliven you.

So players, purpose and goals – all consistent with your values – are necessary for designing a game. Then you establish the basics of a game –

1. the "who" of the game, i.e. the people who are going to be playing the game;
2. the "why" of the game, i.e. the reasons (purpose) for playing the game and the goals to be accomplished;
3. the "when" of the game, i.e. the time you will begin the game and the time when will you end it;
4. the "where" of the game, i.e. the locations/places you will be playing the game (whether it's at home, on vacations, at work, etc.);

5. the "what" of the game, i.e. the rules of the game (remembering that a game is its rules); and
6. the "how" of the game, i.e. the principles for playing the game effectively.

Finally, the design of the game takes into account the characteristics of a game:

- Something that is not happening now is made to be more important than something that is happening – simply by saying so.
- Rules, the allowed paths for attaining what is not happening now, are agreed upon.
- Playing a game is taking actions consistent with the rules. (If your actions are not consistent with the rules, you are not playing the game.)
- All actions result in correlated outcomes or consequences.
- Establishing "positive" consequences is establishing incentives for playing the game fully and attaining its full benefits.
- Establishing "negative" consequences is establishing incentives for returning to the game and it benefits.
- A playing surface or field is agreed upon in the rules, as are measures and a scoreboard or display to see the status of the game.
- A game starts at a specific time and ends at a specific time – sometimes the end is when a specific outcome or score is attained.
- What makes a game fascinating is that there are obstacles to get through, and that you can fail to attain your goals or "lose."

What can you lose in the game called a relationship? Perhaps you could lose the experience of being related; you could lose sight of a relationship being a game; you could lose the benefits of the relationship game; and ultimately, you could lose the experience of owning and being responsible and powerful in your relationships.

Remember – there is no such "thing" as a game. It is created and exists in language. It is made up! It has no inherent significance or meaning, and yet it matters. Playing a game makes a difference.

You have the freedom and the power to co-create relationship games with your partners. You can even play for an extraordinary relationship – which will be the subject of our next book.

Thank you for playing with us by reading this book.

Sandy & Lon

We wish to acknowledge…

… **Our family**, who've been in our lives since we were born, the dearest of all the gifts we've been given in our lifetime. They include our parents, brothers, sister, grandchildren … and, most of all, our daughters, Kirsten and Heidi, who have supported and encouraged us as their parents and as explorers in the wonderful world of families and relationships.

… **Jan Naylor-Smith**, who has been with us since the inception of our work fourteen years ago. Without her expertise in business and technology – and her commitment to families and relationships – there would be no RelationshipByDesign.

… **Carol Herndon and Paul Bennett**, who have engaged with us over the last eleven years – first as curious, adventurous friends and now as our partners and co-creators of the future of our work. In addition, we gladly accepted Paul's offer, as an accomplished author, to assist us in shaping and editing this book.

… **Barry and Penny Berman**, who talked us into braving the field of relationships. They are a living, breathing laboratory for discovering and developing what makes relationships tick.

… **Carol and Jeff England**, who have taken their relationship to heights far and away beyond the ordinary. The results they manifest from their frequent participation in our workshops demonstrate the profound wisdom of paying regular attention to the relationships in our lives.

… **Kristen Moeller**, who had the knowledge and patience to support us step-by-step through the publishing of this book.

... **Adrian Bishop**, whose illustrations in this book capture the often-elusive humor in human relationships.

... **Patricia Stevens**, whose photographs of our workshops helped sustain our dream in its early years.

... **Werner Erhard**, an inspiration for millions of people who have engaged in transformational work since 1971, when he introduced the est training to the world. Our own work with Werner shifted our life's path from making it (as an aerospace engineer and elementary school teacher) to dedicating our lives to the transformation of individuals, families and relationships.

... and finally, **the many courageous, generous people who have participated with us** over these many years, who trusted us and contributed to the evolution of our workshops and explorations. By sharing their experience with others, they supported us in making our work available in the world.

About the authors –

In early 1964, Lon and Sandy had no intentions of writing a book. They were simply college sweethearts who got married so they would have permission to make love, have children, have a home, have successful careers (in aerospace and education), enjoy grandchildren and retire together.

But in early 1974, in a personal development training, they were introduced to a way of thinking and being that shook them to their roots. Seeing that it was possible for them to make a difference in the way people around them experience their lives, they devoted themselves to leading seminars and workshops that made what they experienced available to others.

From the start, Lon and Sandy shared a deep love and appreciation for their families and for the joy and fulfillment that the experience of family brings to life. In 2003, after almost thirty years of working with individuals, they shifted their focus to families and relationships, and RelationshipByDesign was born. Since then, they have designed and led family and relationship workshops and coaching for thousands of people in the United States and Europe. They also have trained others to lead RelationshipByDesign workshops.

Their work, and this book, is based on the insight that no relationship escapes breakdowns. Therefore, there must be something about all relationships that people are unaware of which destines them to disappointment, upset and frustration. When people become aware of their default ways of being related, new ways of relating become available, and people experience a natural freedom, peace and ease in their relationships.

Lon and Sandy live in San Marcos, California, close to their daughters' families, and continue to explore, discover and share the world of relationship, family and community with others.

CPSIA information can be obtained
at www.ICGtesting.com
Printed in the USA
BVHW07s2258100718
521310BV00001B/7/P

9 780998 582351